juunyork

juunyork
The Final Chapter

Brandon McKinney

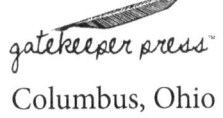
Columbus, Ohio

The views and opinions expressed in this book are solely those of the author and do not necessarily reflect the views or opinions of Gatekeeper Press. Gatekeeper Press is not to be held responsible for and expressly disclaims responsibility of the content herein.

Juunyork: The Final Chapter

Published by Gatekeeper Press
2167 Stringtown Rd, Suite 109
Columbus, OH 43123-2989
www.GatekeeperPress.com

Copyright © 2022 by Brandon McKinney
All rights reserved. Neither this book, nor any parts within it may be sold or reproduced in any form or by any electronic or mechanical means, including information storage and retrieval systems, without permission in writing from the author. The only exception is by a reviewer, who may quote short excerpts in a review.

The editorial work for this book are entirely the product of the author. Gatekeeper Press did not participate in and is not responsible for any aspect of this element.

Library of Congress Control Number: 2022937126

ISBN (paperback): 9781662928222
eISBN: 9781662928239

I am writing this in memory of Junior, the man who showed me I could experience love again. After many failed encounters and one severe heartbreak, this man proved to me that love was worth fighting for. Unfortunately, we only had less than a year together due to a tragic accident. But in that year, we had a lifetime of love and happiness.

Day 1

I wish I could say I met Junior at a store or a restaurant or we had some amazing occurrence where we locked eyes and had a cute awkward encounter, but that was not the case. I met Junior on an app that many of us know all too well in the gay world, "Grindr". One night, I got a message from a very attractive Brazilian man and our sexual preferences seemed to be a good match. We began talking that night for a little bit, but unfortunately I had plans that evening and told this guy to please save me as a favorite and we would circle back. I went to sleep early that night once I got home and moved on to the next day as normal. I worked my normal 8-5 and messaged a few other guys throughout the day on this app. As the evening approached, I had a friend's birthday dinner to celebrate. I never knew that evening, I would be meeting someone who I would fall desperately in love with. However, I would have to go through a few twists and turns before this encounter occurred.

I wrapped up my day at 5:00 o'clock and was planning to celebrate somewhat of a new friend's birthday. The event was occurring around 8:00 that evening. I went to the gym as normal after work and then took a shower and began getting dressed for the evening. I decided to check Grindr again and remembered the attractive Brazilian I was chatting with the night before. I reached out and asked how he was doing. He gave me a quick response. He would be in the Orlando area that evening but would have to go back home that night, which was about an hour away. I responded that I would like to see him tonight, but had a birthday party to attend first, but I would reach out to him that evening. He gave me a thumbs up or some type of quick response to let me know he understood.

I went to attend the birthday party that night. I began driving downtown, which is about 30 minutes away from me. About half way to the event, I realized I had forgotten my driver's license at the gym and had to turn around and travel to the gym first. You will realize throughout this story, I am a bit forgetful and I stress myself out pretty routinely. I would love to say Junior helped me with this, but he was just as forgetful as me and lived his life without much organization or structure.

But anyways back to the birthday event. I finally made it to the club downtown that evening. I provided my ID that I finally had to the staff and entered the party. The party was a great time. I was able to meet a few people and have a few drinks. I posted a picture while at the event and tagged the location. Over the next hour, 2 or 3 guys that lived downtown had reached out to me from that photo asking if I wanted to link up that evening after my party. One was a prior fling that had lasted about 2 months. The other was a guy that I had experimented with prior as well. I know this does not put me in the best light and it makes me seem that I had hooked up with many people. However, the truth was I had been single for almost 2 years and I had met many guys in the Orlando area. As I went to the bathroom, I checked our favorite app and realized another gentleman that I had been talking to prior wanted to see what I was doing that night. I checked to see if the Brazilian had responded or sent any further messages, but he did not.

I ordered one final drink at the event. As you get to know me in this story more, you will not be surprised that I ordered the drink and then ended up spilling it a few minutes later when attempting to take a photo with some friends. At this time, I decided it was probably time for me to leave. I made my way to my car and continued entertaining messages from my social media and Grindr. As I got into my car, I decided to send another message to the cute Brazilian. If you have ever used these apps, you will realize, you typically do not send multiple messages in a row or you come off as that annoying person and you will quickly be blocked or deleted. I wrote a simple message "what are you up to". I received a response pretty quick that he was in the area but pretty tired. I continued responding to some of the other guys, but something inside of me really wanted to meet this one. Physically, he was very much my type and I think that I liked that I had to chase him a bit. As I was heading home, we were chatting back and forth and he advised he would want to see me and I thought for sure he would be coming over. I finally made it home and took a shower and prepped for the event that he would be stopping by.

I do think it's time to explain in the gay world, that it is typical we sometimes will hook up upon meeting each other on this app and typically we are using this app for sexual needs.

I had put on a pair of gym shorts and something that was comfortable in order to meet this guy that I was excited to see. As I finished getting ready, I received a message that he was very tired and would need to go home. I was frustrated at this point and ended up sending one final current picture in hopes that he would come over. Needless to say, it was a bit of a sexual photo. He quickly responded that he was tired, but he now wanted to come over. He said he would be there in 20 minutes or so. I was excited, but I myself was getting a little bit tired as I had drank and also had work in the morning.

    About 30 minutes later, I received a knock on the door. I opened the door and it was this man who had a very aggressive demeanor. I attempted to give him a hug, but it was a bit awkward. We both entered my room and immediately began connecting. I was shocked at our physical connection and his aggression in a way. He was very direct with what he wanted, but it was one of the most sensual experiences I had encountered in a long time. We were physical for almost an hour. He was so dominant and aggressive and that was something I found very attractive. He told me exactly what he wanted done to him and advised what positions he wanted me in for both his pleasure and mine. He was so giving sexually and did many things that were directed at pleasing me which I had not had someone do in a while. Most of the time, guys are more concerned at what is pleasurable to them, but do not focus on the other person involved. However, that was not the case this time. During this sexual encounter, he began kissing my neck and even my face. He would whisper things in my ear that we were very good sexual partners together and that he had not felt this good in a long time.

Before our encounter, we had described things that turned each other on. During this hour, we both continued doing these things to each other and it made the experience so sensual. Upon both of us climaxing, we laid together for about 15 minutes. We both cleaned up in the bathroom and made small talk that this was very fun and that it felt extremely good for the both of us. Unfortunately, again, in the gay world this is somewhat common. We normally will discuss how it was good and that we should meet again, but most of the time we move on with our lives with little response or communication.

As we exited the room, we walked through my living room and we were approaching the front door. I was planning to give him a small hug and let him know to reach out soon, but he stopped me and said, I want to know more about you. I was a little bit surprised and asked what he wanted to know. He said he just wants to talk and to get to know me more. At that time, it was almost midnight and I still had to work early in the morning. I advised him I was pretty tired and maybe we could catch up another day. He said he just wanted to talk for 10-15 minutes and then he would leave. I had never had a guy be so direct and was a bit surprised. We were nearing my kitchen and I said we could talk a little bit if that is what he would like to do. Trying to be clever and ensure this would not be an awkward situation, I advised him we could each ask 10 questions and we both had to answer the questions. I told him he could start. He first asked "What do you do for work?" I provided my answer to him and then asked him what he does. He smiled a little and said, I kind of have a weird profession, but I am trying to become a comedian. I made a joke that it sounded like he does not have a real job. He began laughing so hard and said he had never had anyone be so direct with him before. I smiled and said you were the one who wanted to talk and get to know me.

I then asked him "Where are you from?" He had told me he was from Brazil and then advised that he would take me soon since we have a pretty good connection. I made a joke that he was pretty cocky, but I liked it. I told him about being from the small town of Inverness, Florida. He laughed and told me he had never heard of that before, but since he was going to take me to Brazil, he would take a trip with me to Inverness. He could not pronounce it, and I had to explain how to say it several times. I then told him that the small town of Inverness hosts a pretty spectacular "Cooter Festival." I had to explain to him it was a festival about turtles. Honestly, you just need to Google it to see for yourself. We could not stop laughing through these few minutes.

His next question was very direct. He asked about my past relationships. I was not prepared to go into my major heartbreak that I had, but did tell him about my prior marriage, which was significant in my life as well. I was with a man for 7 years and we were married for one. I told him I was a 26 year old divorced man. He said he was happy I had told him. It became pretty serious at that time and truthfully I was a bit surprised I was explaining this to a man I had just met a little over an hour ago. There were times I hid that information for weeks or months when talking with guys.

We then discussed our favorite foods, favorite color, favorite vacations, and continued talking for an hour I quickly forgot which question we were on and I was loving just talking to you and seeing your passion and smile as you told me things about you. As time progressed, it was almost 2:00 in the morning. We had not moved from my kitchen, where I was sitting on the countertop and you were still standing.

I had told you that I really liked talking with you, but I think it was time that you left because I had to be up soon for work. I went to give you a hug and say goodbye, but you told me that I needed to walk you to the door and give you a proper goodbye because that would mean I plan to see you again. I followed your direction and walked you to the door. I gave you a hug goodbye and you kissed me on the cheek and said that you would wait to see me again. As I went to sleep that night, I could not stop but ponder how unique this evening was.

The Month of July

Some of these details are a bit blurry for me as my phone had shattered in October. If you remember I mentioned I was clumsy, I had actually dropped my phone off a rollercoaster. Without the WhatsApp messages, I will do my best to explain our story. After leaving that first night, you provided me with your phone number and told me that it would be easier for me to text you as sometimes you did not use Grindr and you didn't always keep up with your social media. Little did I know at the time, you had a different reason you didn't like to give people your social media accounts.

Over the next week or two, we would have several encounters where we would be sexually active. However, each time we began spending more and more time together. You would start staying the night and having drinks with me. We would talk so much to each other, but there was always something that I found intriguing about you. You always seemed to be on a mission. Later, I would find out you were chasing this dream of becoming famous here in America, but at the time, you just seemed preoccupied. Each time we hung out, you would make me walk you to the door and say goodbye.

You were so dominant towards me, but you would do it in a soft manner. I remember one evening, you had gotten dressed and I was still in my underwear. I hated walking around in my underwear because I was a bit self-conscious. You told me that I had to walk you to the door because it proved we would get to see each other again. I got up out of bed and I am pretty sure I turned a little bit red in the face. You told me I was so beautiful and you could not believe that you had the chance to keep coming over. This time, we kissed on the lips and began making out as you were leaving. You pressed me against the wall and I remember I felt butterflies in my stomach. After making out, you told me that you would always remember our love story as one that started at 11 PM with you knocking on the door. You also told me that you were a bit jealous and that you didn't want any other guys coming to my door now. I told you that right now, you have been the only person I have been interested in.

The timeline is a bit blurred for me, but on the third or fourth encounter, I caused a little bit of a dilemma for us. I had told you to come over one evening as I was ending work. I realized about 45 minutes into your trip over here that my mom and grandma were also both on the way over to drop off a dryer and bed frame for me. I immediately got nervous as I did not want you to meet my family within the first month of meeting you. I immediately texted you and asked if you wanted to stop somewhere and give me like 30 minutes before coming over so I could do the things with my family and allow them to leave instead of having an awkward encounter. You told me that you did not mind meeting my mom and grandma and thought that would be fun. Inside, I was so nervous because I felt somewhat of a potential with you and I felt this could go extremely wrong. I immediately called my mom and grandma and told them about the situation and advised them to please ensure this was not awkward which I think made it worse as everyone was a little bit on edge at this point.

You made it to my house and I think you could tell I was a bit nervous, but you reassured me it would be fine and that this was my family and that I should not be worried. My mom and grandma arrived and as confident as you were trying to be, I think you were a bit scared. You immediately became very soft spoken and shy. You greeted both my mom and grandma and immediately wanted to show them that you would carry everything in and help them as we set up my bed and dryer. As you began helping them, you initiated small talk with both my mom and grandma. They both kept whispering to me that you were cute and very nice, which made me very shy as well. We all worked towards getting the appliances and items in the house and making the encounter as painless as possible. We were almost in the clear and through the hour-long experience, when we ended up in my bedroom attempting to make the bed after installing the bed frame. My grandmother had seen a bottle of poppers on the end table and asked what it was. You immediately turned red and my mother made a joke that clearly we had been busy on the bed earlier. We all awkwardly laughed and I quickly pushed my family out of the house. I think I knew then you wanted more than just a hook-up.

The month continued to progress and after several times of meeting up at my house, you had told me that you wanted to hang out in public and that this was not just sex for you. We decided one evening to go on a date. We went to CityWalk that evening. I remember you had come over and picked me up in your little car. As we were driving over, you began telling me some personal details about you. You told me that you were supposed to not be "dating" for a while because you wanted to work on your career. You advised me that when you date someone, you typically become fully immersed and can also be very jealous. Part of me (probably something more toxic that I need to look at deeper) really liked that though. I liked the idea that you would fight for me and that you were a little possessive.

That evening we went to a karaoke bar at CityWalk and had dinner and drinks together. It was the first time that it seemed more romantic. We began discussing details about each other that I had not opened up about in a long time to a new love interest. We talked about our families, our coming-out stories, and dug a bit deeper into our past relationships. You were very forthcoming that you also had a tough dating history and did not necessarily believe in forever. You had also told me that you were an extremely sexual person this past year, but you had realized it was a bit unhealthy. You said that almost daily you were meeting guys and it had caused some drama for you in your life as some of the guys were not the most stable.

As we wrapped up the evening, we walked over to the small lake at CityWalk. We held hands for the first time and it was one of the warmest feelings that I had experienced in a long time. You kept making jokes that your friends and family would be laughing if they saw you dating a white guy right now and that this was very unusual for you. We sat by the lake for almost an hour. We did not talk much but still really enjoyed each others company. I remember we took one of our first photos that evening and I had posted it on my Instagram story. A lot of my friends were intrigued as I kept telling them I had met this guy who was different.

As we ended that night, you came back to my house. You had told me that you were going to Brazil for a few weeks, but you had hoped you would be back for my birthday on August 5th. You were supposed to leave that evening, but we ended up falling asleep on the couch together. I fell asleep on your chest and we cuddled all night. Early that next morning, I felt you wake up. I already knew that I had to walk you to the door. We said goodbye to each other and that you would see me soon.

Social Media

I think we should take a pause to discuss social media a bit. I took me a few months to understand how social media would impact our lives. I remember the first time I followed you on Instagram, I noticed you had over 430,000 followers; however you just seemed like Junior to me. We would hang out locally and crowds were not swarming you. Hell, I even felt more popular in Orlando than you.

However, you went on your first trip to Brazil in late July and I began getting calls from friends that were searching for you on the Internet. Some calls were concerning speculation on who you were and your followers. I remember sitting at a pool and some friends had made jokes that I was being catfished and you needed a reason to live in America. Some friends questioned how you became so popular and some friends were amazed by what they found about you. One afternoon as I was driving home, I received a screenshot of your Spotify playlist. My friend was exclaiming that you had songs on Spotify and that you must have been a big deal.

Throughout those weeks that you were gone, I began talking a lot about you to my friends. I was becoming intrigued by what we were finding out. I myself even began to question why you were talking to me. I became intrigued in your life and found myself watching all of your stories and awaiting for you to arrive home. However, the one thing I realized was that I was so happy. I found myself posting things on Facebook that the world seemed to be brighter. The small things around me were bringing me joy. We were talking every day or two and it was cute. I would get excited for your messages and I found myself losing interest in chatting with other guys.

However, the 2 week mark approached and we were discussing my upcoming birthday. From our prior conversation, it seemed like you would be coming back to celebrate my birthday with me. As the day approached, I continued to see you out partying and clubbing in Brazil and I would continue to see other guys in your photos and videos. I began questioning whether you would come home for my birthday and whether the prior month meant more to me than you. On my birthday, you sent me this voice message that I was extremely sweet and that I was different. You told me that you were so glad we had met and that you hoped we could continue to get to know each other. At the time, it hit me kind of hard that you would not be coming home for my birthday.

It made me question whether maybe you were too big of a deal for me. I figured you had all these guys in Brazil going crazy over you due to your popularity and that you may not even be coming back. After my birthday, I began getting a little bit sad. I continued to watch you party and travel throughout Brazil. It felt like our messages were lessening and I did not want to be aggressive in pursuing you as we had only known each other for a month. I began to pull back and figured if you were interested you would look to pursue me.

As the original 2 week trip came to be almost 5 weeks, I began to let go. I found myself going out with friends, entertaining messages from other people, and attempting to live more care-free. I noticed you were reaching out every few days, but it was not consistent anymore. I did not enjoy the feeling of watching your stories anymore as it began to hurt a little bit that I felt you did not care. Then towards the end of August, I received a message that your flight was booked and you were coming home. Even then, I was hesitant on what that meant. I had watched a few of your stories where it appeared you were talking about your ex-boyfriend and past relationships and it did not appear I was a focus for you.

In my head, I imagined that if you were wanting to pursue me, you would look to see me within the first day or two that you were back. As you arrived back into Orlando, it was very late at night. However, throughout that evening you kept giving me updates on what time you were coming home and your travel plans. By 1 AM, I received a text that you were home and that you wanted to see me if I was not too tired. I wanted to play hard to get so bad and tell you I was too tired and that you could come tomorrow because I was a little frustrated that you had been gone so long. However, my heart told me to let you come over.

You continued to share voice messages with me and then shared your location with me. As I watched your location, it felt like my heart was in my stomach. I was so excited for you to arrive. I watched the location as you came closer and closer. Then finally, it showed you parked in my driveway. Inside, my heart was pounding. I had not felt that much passion since the last guy that I was deeply in love with. I opened the door and butterflies consumed my stomach. There you were standing there with that same aggressive demeanor from the first time I met you. However, this time you made a joke that this was a little later than our first 11PM meeting. You broke into a smile and gave me the biggest hug. I don't think I ever told you this, but it was in that moment that I knew I wanted you in my life. Your hug provided such security for me. I felt so comfortable with you. I could have stayed in that hug for hours. However, we ended our embrace and I let you into the living room.

I realized it felt a bit awkward. I felt the emotion towards you, but we were not yet comfortable with each other. We began slowly asking each other questions about the last month as we sat down on the couch. I could tell you looked tired as you had been traveling for almost 15 hours and you looked a bit grungy as well. I asked if you wanted to take a shower and get cleaned up. You accepted and we moved into my bedroom. Immediately as we moved into my bedroom and you began to get undressed, I saw the lighter side of you again. You made jokes about how you were chubbier since the last time I had seen you. You asked if I still thought you were attractive. I made a cute remark that

"We will work with what we have". You showered and then crawled into bed with me.

I do not want to make this a sex story, but I realized after that encounter, our passion was something different. It lasted for almost 2 hours. You began talking very dirty to me and asking me about my fantasies and what I thought about over the last month. You made me open up about desires I had never talked about before but instead would search about on the internet. The physical connection was amazing, but what I found more interesting was how willing I was to open up to you about my sexual preferences. I had never done that before with any partners to the extent that I was doing with you, a guy I only knew for 2 months now. I remember you kept whispering in my ear that we were so compatible and that you have not found a connection like this in such a long time. You would allude to us doing this for a long time together and helping each other satisfy our needs.

As we finished, you fell asleep with me and we woke up the next day. Sexually, we could not stop. We were finding ways to get each other off almost 3-4 times a day. Each time we would get into the house, the chemistry would ignite.

August – Columbus, Ohio

Unfortunately, you do not know me very well, but I am an over-thinker. At this point I was concerned I was feeling too many emotions too soon and began to get scared. I think this may be a good time to share a little bit about that past love I was referencing. When that had ended, I went into a very deep depression. I had even attempted to take my own life at one point. Like I said, this is a different story, but I felt it was important to highlight why I was so scared to trust you and move forward with love again. I was afraid of how it might impact me or cause me to react if things were not to work out.

Upon your return, we spent a day or two together. I had been referencing an upcoming trip that I had to Columbus, Ohio, for a softball tournament but I had not officially extended an invite because many of my friends would be there, including my uncle and my beloved mother and grandmother you had met before. We decided one day to go to lunch at a nice restaurant in the area. At this point, the last 2 days felt so easy. We were spending the entire days together, talking about our personal lives again and I felt like we were really bonding. I thought this would be a good time to ask if you would like to join me on this trip since it would be a total of 9 days and the biggest vacation I would have from work that year.

As we were at lunch, I became a bit nervous to ask as I feared you may reject the offer or I would realize I was asking too much, too soon. As we sat down, we ordered a drink and began opening up to each other. You spent a lot of time at that lunch talking about your family and some of the issues you faced on a daily basis to assist them. You opened up about your mother, who you were having a tough time with as she was battling personal issues for an extended time now. I realized at lunch, you were not the care-free guy that I had thought you were. You had a very hard life growing up and fought extremely hard to make it to your current situation. I enjoyed learning about you and it made me realize how grateful I am for my life. The things that I thought were tough in my life almost seemed like nothing. However, as I told you about some of my problems, you never belittled them. You treated them just as significant as your problems and offered the same sympathy that I had provided you with.

After this honest lunch, I finally spit out the question that I had been trying to get out the entire time. I asked if you wanted to join me on this extended trip to Columbus, Ohio. You seemed a bit surprised and began asking some follow-up questions. You asked who would be there. As I advised, a great deal of friends and even my family would be there, you seemed a bit nervous. You asked about the living situation while we were there. I never told you this but I ended up secretly changing my whole living arrangement to accommodate you because I really wanted to spend the next week with you and attempt to discover if this was really the relationship I wanted to pursue. Ultimately you agreed to the situation and said you would fly out later that evening to Columbus on a cheaper flight to meet me.

Quickly, I scrambled to resolve my living situation. I originally had spent a great deal of money to stay at the hotel that was hosting the event where I would be staying with one of my very close friends in a hotel room. My friend had advised he had no problem if you joined the room with us, but truthfully I wanted the opportunity to spend time with you one on one. As I had said, I wanted to use this time off from work to attempt to discover if this was something special. I ended up paying for my half of the hotel room and then booking a separate Air BnB that I had found 2 days before the trip. There were not many selections left for lodging as this was a country-wide softball tournament. However, I ended up finding us an apartment about 5 minutes from my prior hotel room.

In Orlando, we began prepping for our new upcoming trip. We packed our bags, got our haircuts, and spent the following day preparing. As I told my friends, I would be bringing my new interest, many of them were shocked. I think they had realized this may have been a bit more serious than even they expected. The following morning of August 29th, I set off to Columbus with my mom. I remember telling her I was pretty nervous to be bringing you, but I was so excited we would have this week together.

As I arrived in Columbus and made my way to the Air BnB, I realized this was a situation in which the pictures were a bit nicer than the current situation. I had noticed after settling in, the AC was not working. I quickly became very worried that this was going to be a rough few days if I did not sort this out. I immediately began trying to get in touch with the owner to have this resolved, but they had advised they may not have a solution until the next day.

That evening you flew into Columbus and got an Uber to the AirBnB. As you made it up to the room, I informed you the AC was not working. Luckily, in the evening the temperatures were not too high, so the apartment was actually pretty comfortable. We cuddled up and went to bed together as it was almost 2AM already. As the sun came up, it became very warm in the apartment and we began stripping off the blankets and our clothes. Around 9AM, we both came to the conclusion that it was very hot. I was so nervous about what your reaction would be as we had not really experienced any uncomfortable situations together. You were a bit drowsy that morning, but you hopped in the shower and got dressed to begin the day. The apartment temperatures kept rising and as you got out of the shower, it was almost not comfortable to even continue sitting in the apartment. As you walked out of the bathroom, you did not even seem to notice the temperatures. I gave a big apology that I was so sorry for the AC not working and that I could look to see if we could find another living situation. Inside my head, this was already the second arrangement that had been made, but I really wanted it to work for us.

As I got my apology out, you looked at me like I was crazy. I remember you telling me that we were absolutely not paying for another apartment and that you were from Brazil and this is nothing. You advised we would go enjoy our day and come back to the apartment in the evening once the temperatures cooled down. You advised to let the property manager work on the situation and that we were not going to let this situation have a negative impact on our day. Inside, I was so relieved, typically this situation would have been something that altered many people's moods, but you put me at such an ease. We made our plans for the day and began to have lunch and meet up with friends from my softball team.

That evening, we would attend the opening party where you would again see all my family and this time many of my friends for the first time. What always shocked me as you would meet new people was how shy you would be. I would see this guy on his social media that would be so outspoken and outgoing, but you would meet people and be very nervous. We worked through meeting many people that evening but also worked through many drinks as well. We were both becoming more at ease and I would see you branching out to talk and get to know both my family and friends. I remember that night as being one of the most vivid memories of my life. As the evening ended, we were in this large field at this big party and they were starting a firework show. As the firework show started, we both had our phones out filming. I remember you put your arm around me and said let's turn these off and enjoy the moment. For someone who would be on his phone quite frequently filming, this melted my heart. We sat there and watched the fireworks together and again you had given me butterflies. As we ended the evening, I was pretty drunk. As we stumbled back to the apartment, I hopped on your back and you carried me for a few minutes. You were only about 10-15 pounds heavier than me, so I knew you were tired. I hopped off your back and we made our way back to the apartment. The AC issue still had not been resolved, but there was a window unit in the living room. We cuddled up on the couch together and fell asleep to a Disney movie. We slept all night, embraced together on a couch that was definitely too small for 2 people to sleep on.

Over the next few days, I had days in which I had several softball games, but we would continue to have moments where we would learn more and more about each other. One of the things you loved while in Columbus was the access to electric scooters. You would not take an Uber/Lyft but always find yourself a scooter to ride in on. You quickly became the joke on my team as we would see you pulling up to the softball fields on your scooter and then look to place it in a hidden place in the hopes that no one would take it from you.

One of my favorite things about that trip was that you were interested in getting to know my family and the game of softball. You would sit with my grandma and cheer me on even though you did not understand the objectives of the game. I remember you would take photos of me playing and typically ask basic questions each inning about what was occurring. You began spending a lot of time with my grandma. I remember at the end of one day, you came up to me and said "damn, you would have been so different if your grandma raised you, she has a lot of fight in her." You told me I needed to be more like my grandma so I could get things done in this world. I remember I told you that you probably would not like me if I was like that, and you agreed. You told me that I was right and that my soft side is something that you really enjoy.

I remember throughout that trip, you were meeting many of the expectations that I had set aside in my head for what I wanted. You were taking the time to talk with my family, you were attempting to get to know my friends, and you were consistent in showing up for me. Throughout the week, the AC issue never truly got resolved. We ended up getting a window unit put into the bedroom, but we had come to like hanging out in the living room more. I remember one night, we dragged the mattress into the living room, ordered a ton of chicken McNuggets, got a few drinks and stayed up until 3 AM camping out in the living room. We watched movies and YouTube videos. I remember in my head thinking there was not anywhere else I wanted to be. As I mentioned before, this was a big event in which there were many parties each night, but I found myself just wanting to get to know you better.

I would like to say everything was perfect that trip. But as we were spending every day together, we would bicker about small differences. I remember we had gotten into our first argument one day when we moved fields, and you could not find me when your phone was dying. But we were always quick to make up and continue moving forward.

As that trip came to a conclusion, you began making jokes about what we were, but I am not sure we were technically exclusive yet. I know I had stopped entertaining other messages from people and was not seeking anything out of anyone else.

September

September is probably the hardest month for me to grasp as I mentioned I don't have our WhatsApp messages due to my phone breaking in October. However, there are some key memories I have from September.

As we came back from Columbus, we began spending a great deal of time together. You were still traveling for events almost every weekend and you were basically living out of my house during the weekdays. In September, my friends would see us as a couple and it was no surprise that we would show up together when events would occur. We began attempting to mend our lives together and change the habits that we had built while we were single. One thing that I would continuously do is order Uber Eats or To Go food. You were not a fan of this. I remember in mid-September, after about 2 weeks of to-go food and fast food, you finally said you had enough. You made a joke that we had not used my kitchen since you have been here and you advised you were going to make a home-cooked meal. I agreed that you could go ahead and do so and that I am a terrible cook. You would tell me that you were going to teach me how to cook and I would make jokes that you would not feel useful if I took that from you. Sadly, I never learned how to cook with you, but I would assist in making the salads and prepping the ingredients.

That evening I said I had some meat in my fridge/freezer that you were welcome to use. Around 6:30-7:00 PM, you went to pull the chicken out and you realized the Best By Date was 11/1/2020. You gave me a look that could kill. We laughed so hard in that kitchen that evening as once before I had given you expired chocolate from 2017. That night, you went through my pantry, fridge and freezer and threw away half my food. Sadly, we had another night of Uber Eats.

As I mentioned we were attempting to learn how each other lived and we would bicker and argue about the things we did that bothered each other. I don't recall us getting into any major fights in September, but we definitely were attempting to adjust our habits to be better for each other. I always remember my biggest issue was that you lived an unstructured life, while I had an 8-5 job. On the weekends, you would travel to Puerto Rico, New Jersey, and New York. I remember that was hard for me because during the weekends when I had free time you were typically gone.

As September continued, we kept having our date nights, meeting different friends of mine and getting to know each other further. I remember in late September we did something in Orlando called Magical Dining. For those who don't know, the fanciest restaurants in Orlando offer 3-4 course meals for around $35-$40. One evening I booked us a reservation for an Italian restaurant. I remember as we were getting dressed you made a comment to me that you had never had someone before that you would go on official dates with on a weekly basis. You told me this was one of the most stable relationships you had and it was unique for you to adjust to it. I remember you would apologize to me because you really weren't sure how to dress for a more formal restaurant and it was so easy for me to figure out this type of lifestyle. That night, I gave you one of my dress shirts. After you got dressed, you gave me a hug and thanked me for starting this weekly ritual with you.

We went ahead with our Magical Dining Experience. As we sat down you were very stiff and I remember you telling me that you felt like Jack from the Titanic trying to sort through the plates and silverware. I ordered a glass of wine and you ordered a Sprite. Once the stress of speaking to the waiter and ordering our food was complete, you became more relaxed. I remember you kept making jokes that you felt like I was Beauty and you were the Beast. We laughed through the entire dinner. You would do this thing where you would make up what the other people in the restaurant were thinking. You were so funny, but I never would admit it even though you knew you could make me laugh so easily. My favorite story you made up was a couple that you had thought it was their first date. You had said the guy was not happy with the situation, but he was going to keep drinking until he accepted it because he was about to foot a $100 dinner tab. Another group, there was one rowdy girl in the group. You had made up that all her friends were talking behind her back in the group chat explaining how they are so over Carol and that she does this every time they get together.

We continued to keep going on dates throughout September. I remember one in particular being this cute night I thought I had planned at Disney Springs. We were going to go watch this movie at the Dine-In Theater. When we arrived, we realized we had to buy masks to go into any of the establishments. We walked over to the vending machine and bought the needed masks. Upon finishing, I went to throw away the wrappers from the mask and realized I had thrown away my credit card as well. I looked at you in embarrassment and had to tell you what I did. You smiled at me and walked over to the trash can. You realized you could not reach anything and had to take off the lid. As you were trying to reach for the credit card, people around you began looking and smirking. When you finally obtained the card, 4 or 5 people had stopped. We both could not stop laughing that dating me leads to dumpster diving. I thought that was the end of misfortunes for the evening; but then we entered the theater. The movie started and about 15 minutes into the movie, we realized this was a full-on musical in which they would not stop singing. When reviewing the movie on my own, I had not realized they would be singing the entire time. About 25 minutes into the movie, we both looked at each other and realized we would rather walk out than watch that entire movie. After leaving, we could not stop laughing at how bad this date was. We then finally went to get ice cream and sat on the bench eating sundaes laughing at the fact that I was never allowed to choose the movie again.

Towards the end of September, you had advised me that you were pretty sad that you had a little dog that was staying in a kennel since you had moved out of your prior house and currently did not have an official lease at this time. You had told me that you did not want to tell me about her because you didn't want any expectation that I would help take care of her because you knew that was the type of person I was. One weekend afternoon, I had gone and walked around Lake Eola. You had advised that you had taken the dog out of the kennel for a few hours. I had told you to bring the dog by so I could meet her. As I was sitting on the ground at Lake Eola, I saw you carrying this little 5 or 6 pound dog up to me. You set her down and she immediately came wobbling up to me. We sat outside for about an hour with the dog, which I would learn was named Lexie. She was so happy to be in the sun and be around people. As we wrapped up the afternoon, you told me you were going to take Lexie back to the kennel and then come over for lunch.

I had told you that I wanted to spend more time with the little dog and told you to take her over to my house. You did not want to do this and you felt it was too much for me to have Lexie at my house. After a little bit of debating, you agreed to take Lexie over to my house and we all spent the afternoon on the couch together watching movies and eating lunch. She stayed right on top of your chest and was so happy to be with you. Since that day, Lexie never went back to that kennel. Today, as I am writing this, she sits next to me and her presence makes me still feel like you are here as well.

As September came to an end, you had advised me that you would need to go back to Brazil for 2 weeks or so to help your mom with some personal issues that she was having. I would say these next few months mark when passion really erupted for us.

October

As October began, there was not a doubt in my mind that I wanted you in my life. There were many confusing factors for me to sort through though, one of them being your social media presence. I really struggled watching you on social media as you were traveling because sometimes I felt more like a fan than a love interest. As you arrived back in Brazil, you immediately began connecting with your friends and family, which was expected. I also kept myself busy with friends and family, but we would have many instances where drama and jealousy would erupt. There were times you would become angered if I did not respond in a timely manner and I really struggled seeing you out at bars and clubs because I could only imagine the amount of people interested in you and wanting to spend time with you, especially in a sexual way.

The sexual thoughts were a struggle for me because I knew how sexual of a person you were and I only figured that you were doing things on your own while traveling. However, we pushed through the first 2 weeks or so and I tried to think positive and think that you would be back shortly to be with Lexie and I. One of our most recurring fights on that trip was that you were supposed to be home a lot sooner than you actually were, just as your first trip. You would keep advising me that you would be home in 2 or 3 days, but the days kept passing and the deadline kept getting further and further away. I had noticed one guy in particular that kept popping up in your stories that was not a family member. I had seen him coming out of a hotel with you one morning and then even traveling over 15 hours to your home city with you. I quickly became jealous as I recognized this.

Deep inside, I was so hurt. I remember one morning being almost in tears thinking that maybe you had someone in Brazil that you were dating as well. The fact that we did not have an official status made it even harder for me. As we continued to talk over the next day or two, you would advise me you were just spending time with your family. One morning I ended up finally breaking, advising that you must really like the guy you were with because I had seen him in your videos for a few days now and it appeared he had traveled across the country with you. I myself was so damaged from my last heartbreak, and the only thing I knew how to do was run. I blocked you on social media and had advised when you get back you can get Lexie from here and move on. I brought up that you had not mentioned this guy when we spoke, but he clearly was someone that you were spending days and nights with. You became very defensive and began searching for me on your private social media account. You sent me several voice messages advising me how you knew the guy and advised that I needed to call you immediately to talk with you. I called you later that evening and apologized for being so dramatic and hurt. I told you I was really scared, that I thought I liked you and I was not sure I could go through the pain of another heartbreak. You reassured me how you knew the guy and even gave me his social media information and asked if I wanted to talk to him.

I regretted how I acted and apologized to you. I expressed my frustration that you were still not home even though you kept telling me this would just be a two week trip. You advised you would be home soon and within a few days you gave me the flight information for your return.

When you did return, the first night, we began exploring further sexual interests. As we were having sex you began asking me about my fantasies. You asked me if I had done anything while you were gone. At first I did not know how to respond. I assumed you were doing things since we were not official, but I did not want to break trust or hurt you either in the case that you were not. But you kept pushing; you told me to tell you everything I did. I told you that I did hook up with someone from my past during the past month. I quickly realized this was a turn on for you. You began asking what he did to me and what I liked. I had told you about the guy and even how big he was. You began getting even more passionate with me and it was such a turn on for you. You had told me that I am allowed to do things with other guys, but I had to get your approval first because I am yours. It was so hot for me to have someone so turned on by this. I attempted to see if you did anything while you were in Brazil, but you were not very forthcoming. I had left it alone because I had felt we had made a pretty big step already in what we shared.

Puerto Rico – October

As you came back from your trip to Brazil, I had advised that I wanted to do something fun with you as it had been almost a month since we were together. We planned a trip to Puerto Rico the following weekend. This weekend we would have one of our 3 largest fights. We would leave on October 29 after I had finished work. Your social media presence was becoming tough for me as I was beginning to feel excluded. You would consistently be posting live videos and even when I was there you would avoid me from being in the video. It began to hurt my feelings because at that time you would call me your boyfriend, but it felt like you were still attempting to hide me.

That night before departing we got into an argument concerning your social media as you were in the airport making videos and I was sitting at the terminal by myself. After you realized I was frustrated, you came and sat down with me and I apologized for what you were doing. You had told me you would stop making videos today and we would enjoy our flight to Puerto Rico. It was hard because I did not want you to stop doing what you loved, but I also did not want to feel excluded either. That evening we arrived in Puerto Rico. The hotel was beautiful. We had a few drinks at the hotel and went to sleep pretty early. The next morning we would wake up to experience a full day in Puerto Rico.

Upon waking up, we went and got lunch by the beach. We then spent the day by the pool and had a few drinks. As the drinks were progressing, we were getting very sexual. I had asked you if you wanted to include someone else in our sexual experience that afternoon/evening, but you told me adamantly "no". Our connection sexually was continuing to grow and each encounter was becoming more and more passionate. After waking up from a nap, we decided to go out for the evening to the clubs. We actually up to this point had not been to a club together. We got dressed for the evening and went downstairs to the lobby. The lobby was hosting a big Halloween event. You actually had promoted the hotel on your Instagram story and they had shared it on their story as well. Upon leaving the hotel, we walked through their major event in the lobby and one of the photographers had asked to take our photo on the backdrop they had set up. You had told me that you did not want to take any photos, but I had urged that we take one together just on my phone. You had given me an attitude that you didn't want to share any photos tonight. I then went to the bathroom and we went to find dinner together.

I had suggested we go to a nice restaurant, but you had told me that you wanted me to see true Puerto Rican culture. You took me to an area about 20 minutes from the hotel where we ate at food trucks. It was so nice to be immersed in the culture. In the area with the food trucks, many families and kids were dressed up for Halloween. We sat at a picnic table outside next to this other family and you were chatting with the family as we had dinner together. It was one of my favorite things about traveling with you. I felt like you were always wanting to see the true cities and not the tourist attractions. Upon finishing dinner, we were headed to the car and I noticed while I was in the restroom earlier you went and took a selfie at the same backdrop and posted it on your social media. It made me very angry that you had told me you did not want to post any photos, but then when I stepped away you did so.

    We got into the same recurring argument that you were trying to hide me from your followers and your world. You would try to explain to me that you wanted to keep our life private and that it had disrupted relationships in your past, but it was hard for me to understand. The way I saw it was that you were hiding me from your social media so you could be open to pursue other things. We continued arguing in the car and as we were growing passionate, our arguments were typically more heated. As we parked the car and made our way to the club, things kept escalating on the street. We were beginning to get loud with each other and I could tell you were becoming upset; however I was not willing to let go because this was something that really was hurting me. As we were walking in the street, you had a corona bottle in your hand. As we began to yell at each other, you finally exclaimed that you had enough and shattered the beer bottle in the street. People had noticed which made me even angrier. I walked away to go back to the car but you really wanted us to go have a fun evening at the club. I told you if we went into that club and continued drinking, we were going to end up fighting even more. After 30 minutes of arguing in the streets we finally made it back into the car. I went back into the hotel room that evening and in my head I did not think that we could be together if you were not willing to accept me publicly as your boyfriend.

That next morning, I woke up before you. I went and got breakfast and went and sat by the pool. You began calling me to speak to me. We both went over what was hurting us and you kept advising me that you were not ready to make our relationship public as it has caused you issues in the past. I did my best to accept it, but I was still hurt. That morning we agreed to have a fun last day in Puerto Rico.

I suggested we go zip-lining, but just as the day before, you did not want to do tourist activities, you wanted to take me to see the real Puerto Rico. We got in the car and drove to the beach. We would stop frequently on the side of the street to buy local food and drinks. It was such a beautiful day. As we approached the end of the beach, it seemed like a normal beach, but then you advised you had a surprise for me. You walked me into the woods, which I have to admit now scared me a little bit. We walked through the woods for almost 5-10 minutes where we came out almost on the edge of a cliff. It was the most beautiful thing I had ever seen. We were overlooking the water and we had the entire mountainside to ourselves. We began exploring the side of the cliff and climbing down near the water. You took some pictures with me and I remember you made a joke that you still were not going to share these on your social media, but this would be a reminder for us of this beautiful moment.

We then climbed down into a cave together. At this point, we were becoming very sexual with each other. We began making out in the cave. You then wanted me to pleasure you in the cave as you recorded it. It was one of the most exhilarating moments of my life. I had never been in such a beautiful and more passionate setting. Up until this point, I think that was the most passionate moment I had ever felt. Once we ended at the beach, we then made our way back to the hotel to relax before boarding our plane that evening.

At the hotel, you finally agreed to jump in the pool. You did not know how to swim and I was instructing you from the sidelines on what to do to float. You were like a little kid trying to learn something new. I sat and watched you as you would hold your breath underwater and experiment trying to learn how to navigate a pool. I saw such an innocent side of you and recorded this experience without you knowing. Even with our arguments that weekend, I was in paradise.

As we were headed back to the airport, we again were becoming sexual and passionate. We had the rental car and you advised you wanted to be dirty one more time in Puerto Rico. We pulled into an abandoned parking lot and used the rental car to experiment with each other. Hindsight, I am just happy we both did not end up in jail in Puerto Rico. It was a trip I will remember for the rest of my life.

November

As I look back at November, I would describe this month as our growing pains. At this point you were fully moved in with me and we were trying to adjust our lives to fit each other. We also were battling exclusivity and some of your own financial issues. I would learn that every time you would make money, you would have to figure out how to split it to ensure you were assisting your family. I would continue to fall deeply for you as I learned about the battles you faced on a daily basis to ensure you were providing support for your family.

One day I got so scared I lost Lexie. I was panicking while going through the house and after almost 15 minutes, I had found her in my closet in my underwear box on the floor. I remember I had told you when you got home where she was. You had explained to me there was a period of time in which you had slept in a closet for a few months. It really broke my heart, to hear some of the things you had to go through. I remember that evening you told me that this was probably the best living situation you had ever been in. Even though I think we argued the most this month, I think I learned the most about why you were the way you were. You were used to being a loner and having to fight for yourself. Just as I was having commitment issues, you were also tackling how to accept me into your life. I will admit I am not easy to deal with as well. I am very organized and can sometimes be controlling. So many times we would have to apologize for our misunderstandings and I remember you would advise me that we grew up in two very different cultures and it was okay that we were fighting. I remember you telling me that relationships are typically very passionate in Brazil.

During this time, we also began building a routine. We would eat dinner together more often and go the gym daily together. You continued conducting your events for social media. You were very excited about being able to host a reality show in November. I would later find out a lady from New York hosted this event with you. She would become someone who fought so hard for you after your life ended to ensure you made it back to Brazil.

We also were beginning to explore things sexually, which was very exciting for me. Never in my life had I had a relationship like this where we tried so many new things. In the first few weeks of arriving home, we began experimenting with my submissiveness. We would try blind folds, role playing, and many other things. You also began to allow me to hook up with other guys that you had approved of. You would make me record the experiences and we would watch them together as this was a big turn on for you. You experienced such pleasure in seeing me dominated. This further deepened our passion as both of us had admitted that we had not done this before in prior relationships. One of the things we never could really sort through was planning for a third person to be involved.

We both would end up getting jealous and there were times we would cross the lines with each other when attempting to find someone else.

We were definitely experiencing that passion and aggressiveness with each other. We had one fight that we got so mad at each other and neither of us were willing to budge. You thought I was out partying with my friends. I had thought you were out somewhere where you were not supposed to be. You did not have the spare key with you and you ended up falling asleep outside my front door because you were too stubborn to talk to me. The whole time I was inside the house because I did not want to admit I was at home waiting for you. I woke up at 4AM to find you sleeping outside. I pulled you inside and put you in bed. We cuddled up with each other and that night I cried quietly because I was becoming so scared at how much I had fallen for you.

About a week later, we had gotten into another fight over the glorious Grindr app. I had come home and was so infuriated at what I had found and how it did not follow the agreement we had set up. I was the most aggressive I had ever been in my life. I shattered a plate full of pasta across the house and began launching all of your stuff at the front door. I was shaking in anger and I had made the decision that afternoon that we needed to come to an end. I left for the day to spend some time alone. I found myself crying by the lake that I allowed myself to fall so hard for someone again and it was truly scary for me. We began apologizing to each other throughout the day via text, and by the time I made it home, we began working to make up with each other. As angry as we would be with each other, we never wanted to leave each other alone. I would later find a note you wrote to me apologizing when you were planning to leave the house that night in which I hid because I thought one day we would get to laugh about it.

As we ended in November, you had the opportunity to interview a big star from Brazil. I loved seeing you send me the photos and videos from this experience. You were a natural interviewing him and I just know if you got to be in this world a little bit longer, you would have been able to be famous not just in Brazil, but here too. I remember you had invited me on this trip, but it was Thanksgiving and I was going home to spend time with my family. I remember that I had sent you photos of Lexie on Thanksgiving from my grandparents. You told me that she was now living like royalty compared to what she had prior.

December

One of my favorite memories from December was when we had a gingerbread building contest. I had gone to Publix to get 2 gingerbread house kits for us. When I got home, I still do not think you fully understood what I wanted to do. I had explained that we would each have 1 hour to build a gingerbread house and then we could share them on our Facebook and Instagram and have our friends vote to see who built a better house. We laughed so much completing this together. Again, you had advised how different this was from your past relationships. I sat on the ground and built mine as you sat at the kitchen table. When we first started, you weren't showing too much interest. But when you saw how quickly I began to build mine, you started to get competitive. We began both laughing and making fun of each other as we progressed. You could not get yours to stand up properly and I was not letting you live it down. After 1 hour, we stopped. We had taken photos of both our houses which were both pretty rough. I am still not positive who was considered the winner even after the votes. But it was so fun to begin experiencing the holidays with someone again.

The following week we would plan a trip to Las Vegas together. I like to say this was when we finally found our groove together. Las Vegas was the best vacation I had taken in my entire life. We were so focused on each other during this trip and ensuring that we were both treating each other correctly. We took a night-time flight to Vegas after one of my shifts at work. We landed in Vegas pretty late. During our first night we had the funniest moment in our relationship, at least in my opinion. Since edibles were legal in Vegas, we had found some to consume upon our arrival. We decided to take one and head to the casino downstairs. As we were hanging out in the casino downstairs, I think the edible started to do its job. As we were losing in the casino, we both had imagined we were spending big money. After what felt like hours of losing in the casino, we both got frightened that we had blown thousands of dollars. I still recall at the end of the evening, I did not think we would even have the money to get home from Vegas. That next morning we woke up and realized, we had spent about $15 each. All night, we were playing on the change machines. We both could not stop laughing that morning at how dramatic we were.

You had never been to Vegas, so we spent a day sight-seeing together and enjoying some of the monuments that they have in Vegas. I still have one of the photos of us together sitting right next to me. We both were so calm during that trip and worked to ensure we allowed each other to enjoy what we both wanted. One of the nights, we decided to go to one of the gay clubs in Las Vegas. If you recall from Puerto Rico, we still had never been to an actual club together, now, almost 5 months after dating. That night we got dressed up together and decided to make our way down to the club. We entered the club and started having a few drinks together. The club was set up very uniquely with several different rooms. We began navigating the different rooms. Your favorite one was the Latin one, and we found ourselves dancing together in that room. That was actually the first time we had ever danced together. You were so dominant and I found such comfort in being in your arms.

As the night progressed, we were drinking more and more. We both had noticed other guys trying to get our attention as we navigated through the club, but neither of us were giving anyone else any attention. Towards the end of the night, I went to the bathroom. As I came out, I saw you talking to two attractive guys. They seemed to be interested in you. As I walked up, they both had advised me that they were fans of yours and could not believe you were out. I was surprised that you had fans in Las Vegas. As I approached, you put your arm around me and introduced me as your boyfriend. My heart had sunk because this was the first time you ever called me your boyfriend to someone else. It was approaching almost 1:30AM and I had told you I was getting tired. You began to make fun of me because you said people party in Las Vegas until 5AM. You ordered the Uber back to our hotel. In the Uber, you were telling the Uber driver, you still wanted to party, but you were being a good boyfriend and coming home with me because I was tired. The Uber driver found us very cute and had advised it was nice to see you willing to come home with me so early. She also made fun of me for wanting to go to bed so early and she advised I had a very good boyfriend for being such a team player. I kissed you in the Uber that night and told you "I love you" for the first time.

The final morning in Vegas, we went to brunch with unlimited mimosas. This would be the first time you had posted a video of me on your Instagram. You had told me all your followers wanted to know who I was, but you were happy that we had such an amazing weekend together. We flew home that evening and I still say that was the best vacation I have ever been on with a significant other.

As December came to an end, you would make your final trip to Brazil for Christmas. Before leaving, we exchanged Christmas gifts with each other. I had taken a photo from Vegas that we took together and had it blown up and placed into a frame. One morning when you woke up, I gave you both the photo and a card. That morning you teared up. You made a joke to me that I better keep that photo in my living room for the rest of my life, even if something happens to us, because it was the perfect photo. You gave me a big hug and kissed me on the forehead. You ended up getting me one of my favorite colognes for Christmas and also a Christmas card. As I dropped you off to head to Brazil, you started to get very emotional with me in the car. You had told me that you never expected to fall for me as much as you have. We could not stop kissing each other that day as I dropped you off at the bus station to head to Brazil.

Unfortunately, as with most of your trips to Brazil. The trip had become extended longer than what you said. We had a few days we would argue on this trip concerning when you were coming home and I remember there was even a night I told you to stay in Brazil because I was so upset. However, we did have a very magical moment on New Year's Eve. We both had agreed to call each other at our prospective midnights. I called you first when midnight struck in Brazil. We facetimed together and wished each other a Happy New Year's. You then called me right after New Year's struck in the United States and wished me a Happy New Year's as well.

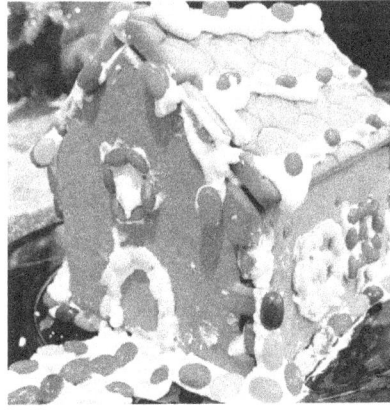

Juunyork: The Final Chapter

January

You were in Brazil for most of January. Some of my favorite messages you would send me were photos of your nieces and nephews. We had made jokes that this was what our kids would look like one day. We had talked about you wanting several kids a few times. We always said you would be the tougher parent and I would be the pushover parent. It was the first time in my life that I had imagined having a family with a partner of mine. I think you would have been an amazing dad. You always would light up around kids and have such a soft side. I used to love to even watch you interact with Lexie. You had such a way of bringing happiness to both children and animals.

I remember towards the end of your trip, you had sent me a video of the monuments in Brazil that you had a tattoo of. You had promised we would take a tour of them together. You had such pride in your home city.

February

I would say February was one of our most beautiful months and unfortunately our last full one together. We were working together as a team and communicating very well. However, it was a month in which you began experiencing financial struggles. You were trying extremely hard to find ways to send your family money. You would take your first trip with a trucking company. I remember you had told me that you loved trucking and the chance to travel and make your video content. However, on your first trucking trip, they had given you a truck that had engine/ignition issues and you found out the vehicle could not travel more than 60MPH as you were driving. I remember the truck had broken down in Gainesville on your way home the weekend before Valentine's Day. Someone from the trucking company had to assist in traveling out there to fix the truck and ensure you made it home. I remember when you got home we discussed you would not travel with that truck again. You had told me that the company advised that they were in the process of fixing another truck for you to take out at a later time. You would not travel again for almost 2 weeks until the company notified you that they had a different truck for you to use.

One of my favorite times in February for us was Valentine's Day. I remember the night before you left the house for like 2 hours. I remember I was watching a movie and decided to call you because it seemed to be a while. You ended up calling me back about 15 minutes later and I opened the door to see you standing there with roses, chocolate and balloons. My heart had melted. I knew you were not the most romantic person and to see that you spent the time to do this for me really meant a lot.

For you, I had bought tickets to a dinner show. I remember I had gotten off work and we had our reservation. We began making our way to the event when you recognized I had put in the wrong address. We laughed that this was becoming pretty typical for our relationship. We put in the correct address and finally arrived with little time to spare. The dinner show was probably one of my favorite dates with you. I remember we sat down at a table for 2 and you seemed to be a bit awkward with how intimate the setting was. However, we both ordered a drink and began the night. Throughout the dinner show, the hosts would have the couples stand up and say things to each other. They would have us dance, hold hands, and kiss. We laughed and participated together. Being one of the only gay couples at the dinner show, I think a few couples around us found us to be very cute. One offered to take our picture together.

As the show progressed, the hosts had asked for volunteers to participate. They were walking through the theater area and as they walked by us, the hosts had pointed at you to come on stage. You were extremely nervous and had told me to go up due to the language barrier. I had told you "no way" and they most likely were going to have you sing or dance, and that was something you were much better at than me. After giving me a very dirty look, you went on stage. You introduced yourself to the hosts and of course they would have you perform a dance for the crowd. You were a natural, the crowd began cheering, and you even received a standing ovation from some people. After your first dance, they then had you perform a strip tease for the audience, which again you were a natural. You came back to your seat and you were proud that you did so well. As we ended the evening, you would tell me this was the best Valentine's Day you have ever had and then make a smart remark only because you do not typically celebrate it. I have celebrated them all my life and it was by far my best. I wish I would have said that to you.

After this we would only have 10 more days before you went on your next trip with your trucking company. I am so grateful that our last 20 days together were so peaceful. We had dinners together nightly, we went to the gym, and we helped complement each other's lives. We had 1 night where we met up with about 10 friends and had a blast at one of the local gay bars. We played pool, we drank, and we laughed so hard. One of my favorite things that we would do when we hung out was sing in the car together. We had grown to be so comfortable with each other. I remember you would pretend like your hand was a microphone and make me sing into it. You would say "Ladies and Gentlemen, please prepare for the next performance." As much as I am sad that things have ended, I am grateful for the final memories we had together. It was a time in which we found pure happiness with each other.

During our final weekend together, we made a trip to Sea World with some friends. You were not used to hanging out with a lot of gay guys, so I remember it was always a bit of an adjustment for you because I typically would plan things in larger crowds. We experienced many new things at Sea World together. We rode roller coasters, saw the shows, and had a beautiful moment together sitting in one of the park areas. At this time, we started to know unique things about each other. I am horrible with names and I typically would introduce you as an excuse to have the people around us say their names. I remember at Sea World, we walked by this couple and I was trying to get you to introduce yourself to one of the people in the couple. You did not catch along and quickly part of the couple became upset that I did not remember their name. As we walked away, you busted out laughing that you forgot to do your job.

I have contemplated telling the story of what happened that evening, but I think it is something I do want to talk about. As we got home, we were a few drinks in. In the last few days, we had tried to initiate being intimate, but I was typically too tired and would have to go to bed early. That evening, I really wanted to do something different and find a way to please you. I had come up with the idea to find someone on Grindr for us to experiment with. As I was searching, I realized my stomach was bothering me, but I still wanted to find someone for you. I was very nervous at the idea, but it was something I had never done with anyone before. I decided to search for someone for you and made the decision to invite them over. We both became extremely nervous but it was something I was urging you to try especially since in the past I had been with people without you.

Before the person came, you had told me that you wanted to please me, and we had done some things to accomplish this before the person arrived. As we continued our communication with the other person, we had made the decision to tell them you had a roommate just in case they heard anyone in the house. As the person arrived, I went into my bedroom and you took the person into the spare bedroom. Being honest, I was not sure how I felt, but I decided to go into the living area to become more involved in the situation. As I heard you being pleasured, it quickly became one of the best sensations I have ever felt. In a short timeframe, I pleasured myself 3 times. I was shocked at my reaction to this, but it was such a big turn on for me. As you concluded, I heard you say goodbye to the other person and walk back into our bedroom. You seemed to be very nervous at my reaction, but I explained to you that it was honestly one of the hottest things I had ever done sexually. I advised that as long as we continued to prioritize our intimacy and that you do not communicate secretly with people, I would not mind doing it again. Two nights later, we were intimate ourselves. It was by far the most passionate experience we had together. You had talked about wanting to complete that experience with me and also you doing it again as well. I think because we were being so honest and open about our needs and how to accomplish them, it brought us even closer together.

We would attempt to create that experience again before you left on your final road trip, but ended up not being able to. The last few days we had together were extremely peaceful. You began prepping for your next trip. I had given you an extra blanket to keep you warm. I had also gone to Publix to purchase you additional energy drinks and water as well to make sure you did not get sleepy.

One of the things that I am most grateful for is that the last words I said to you face to face were "I love you and travel safe". You kissed me on the forehead that evening and went to begin your road trip.

Over the next few days you would talk about how you missed me and that you could not wait to come home. We sometimes would fight when you would leave for jealously reasons, but thankfully we did not have a single argument this time. We would check in on each other, call each other, and wish each other well each day. I actually for the first time sent you a voice message, which I was so embarrassed about. I would hate hearing my voice, but I did it for you because you would send them to me daily.

Juunyork: The Final Chapter

Juunyork: The Final Chapter

The Last Day

I will remember this as the most horrifying 24 hours of my life. That evening at 10:25 you messaged me asking if I could pick you up that night. You explained the truck had broken down again but they were almost done with fixing the tire and you should be home around 2:30 or 3:00 that night. About 30 minutes later, I gave you a call to confirm your arrival time and you did not answer. In the message you mentioned you may be stopping at a rest stop to sleep, so I did not think too deeply into it at the time. I called several times to follow up and ended up lying down for bed around midnight. At 4AM, I woke up to use the restroom and messaged you again asking for an update. I did not hear from you. When I woke up that morning around 9:30 AM, I began to panic.

I had actually reached out to 2-3 friends to understand their opinion on the situation. You had always told me that you wake up with the Sun when you are driving the truck because it was so bright. By that time in the morning, the Sun was already out. I was wondering why I had not heard from you. I had asked one of my friends if they thought I should call the police, but they had recommended giving you a few hours in case your phone was dead or maybe even broken. I had two softball games that afternoon and decided to go to them to try and stop staring at my phone. However, each inning I kept checking and almost called every 30 minutes. By the end of my 2 games, I had gone over to my mom who was playing on another field. At that time, I was in a panic. It was almost 1:30 PM. It felt like I had called a dozen times and I did not know what to do. I had advised her I wanted to call the police. She recommended I check at home just to ensure you had not made it home and possibly your phone was just broken. As I was driving home, it felt like the longest drive. At that time, the worst case scenario I could imagine was that you were in a hospital somewhere hurt.

I finally arrived home. It felt like I was driving for hours. You still were not home. My heart went into my stomach. I kept trying to figure out how to be logical now. I sat down at the counter and mapped out every hospital between Savannah, Georgia (your last known location) and Orlando, Florida. I began calling each hospital and as I would spell out your name, I would receive a response each time that you had not been admitted. I was a bit relieved each time, but also a bit stressed that I still did not understand your location. I began calling both the Florida and Georgia police departments but kept getting bounced around. One department advised you were located in Georgia and I needed to call Georgia. The other department advised I lived in Florida and needed to call Florida. Each time I would be given a new number and directed to call someone else. I remember one lady being quite helpful and taking down your information to attempt to follow up on any accidents, but she was unfortunately unable to assist. The final call I made was to a non-emergency department where I was directed to leave a message in which I tried to provide all your information. At that time, I felt like I did everything I could.

I was sitting in my house for almost 30 minutes and I was just in a panic. I felt so helpless. I knew it was my grandfather's birthday celebration that day. Each year we would both assist each other in blowing out our candles on our birthday cakes. I felt it would be good for me to go and also not feel so helpless. I drove to the Villages at this time to celebrate my grandfather's birthday. By the time I arrived, it was approximately 6:00 PM. As I walked into the room for dinner, I knew my mom had told everyone already about the situation. I immediately began to tear up and just tell everyone that I did not know what to do. I began sharing my most recent messages with you with my family and they began to offer their advice. By this time, more than 14 hours had passed since you were supposed to be home. I decided to dig through my messages and find the emergency contacts you had listed for me. I messaged all these numbers including two of your other friends. I had asked everyone if they had heard from you, but each person would respond that they had not talked to you since the day before. My heart just kept getting heavier with each minute. By this time, each one of my family members was attempting to google different police departments and try to offer their assistance. I had advised we should do my grandpa's birthday cake since I felt like I had taken over his whole party. We all sang "Happy Birthday" and took our annual photo of assisting each other with the candles. Directly after singing, we each went back into the search for you.

My brother had called me as he works for dispatch; he attempted to give me advice on how to get this incident reported correctly. As we were attempting to report the incident again, one of your friends, Dany, whom I would later appreciate very much, sent me a possible article concerning an incident in Georgia. The first few sentences of the article describing an unknown death brought me into a panic. As I attempted to read further, I had noticed it described a large yellow Penske truck. I set the phone on the counter in relief that it was not you. My mom was behind me also reading the article, and as she continued to read it, she had noticed it involved a white Ford F-350. She asked to see the article and then I heard her inform my grandparents, this death is involving a white truck. I immediately became hysterical. The one thing I could not even imagine seemed to be possible. I remember just dropping to the floor and sobbing. My grandfather who is 73 years old, dropped to the floor with me and just held me as I began screaming.

I remember my mom in the background calling to follow up on the article and demanding to speak to someone involved in the case. Things at this time were a bit blurry and I just remember my grandfather wrapped around me advising that he was so scared and that he would be here for me no matter what. I remember both he and my grandmother also began crying and I remember they seemed to be scared I would not be okay. I knew they were aware of my suicide attempt several years ago. I think that began to cross their minds as I was hysterical for an extended period of time. It seemed like hours for my mother to confirm what had happened. I knew she had stepped into another room to begin trying to confirm the details. I remember just screaming to ask her if it was you. Finally, after what felt like forever, she had confirmed it was you. For the next 30 minutes, I just remember being in between anger and extreme sadness.

As I finally calmed down and looked at my phone again, I had seen many of your family members begin to question where you were. At this point, I knew I had to get home and attempt to be with my friend who spoke Portuguese so I could properly explain to your family what happened. I could not send a translated text that their son, brother, best friend, was now dead. As my mom and I were driving back to Orlando, my friend immediately advised he was on his way. I also asked your friend, Dany, who I had never met to please come over as I knew we would need to explain this to several people.

I remember as I drove home, I felt like I was outside of my body. This seemed unreal. I had not even fathomed death as an option for you. The text message I will never forget from your little brother, Pablo, stated "please find my brother." I broke down again as I read this message and I knew you were gone. As I approached home, your friend Dany, who I never met before, was in my driveway. I opened the car door and broke down into her arms. We both cried in my front yard at the news. As we got inside, my other friend had arrived as well. I remember just sobbing and attempting to explain what had occurred to you so they could relay this information to your family and friends. As the calls began, I remember just hearing screams and cries on the other end of the phone. It felt like someone just kept stabbing me in the chest with each phone call. Finally, it felt like we had gotten the news out to all the needed parties. I remember just sitting in silence for an extended time. Everyone just seemed lost and broken. We began trying to talk about what happened and what we needed to do.

To be honest, I don't think anyone understood what to do until we obtained the next steps from the detective. I finally asked my friends to leave the house as I was just mentally exhausted and felt shattered. I could no longer keep trying to talk about what had happened. I honestly just wanted this day to be over. To be honest, I didn't even want to wake up again without you being here.

I remember I laid in bed with Lexie and just kept sobbing. I began listening to messages from you throughout the last week. I could not fall asleep. Around 5AM, I moved over into the spare room where my mom was. My phone kept going off with questions from your family as they tried to piece together what had occurred. I felt obligated to respond. I remember my mom had told me to place my phone on silent and attempt to sleep for an hour or two.

The next morning, I woke up and I had asked your friend Dany to please come over again to help answer the questions from your family. She was already awake and advised she would be over shortly. As she arrived, she sat me down and explained that this may be the last thing I wanted to do, but she advised that the news had been released in Brazil, that you were dead. She said that many people would look to create funds or accounts to assist you, but if the right people were not involved, money and funds could be incorrectly raised for you. That morning we established a "Go Fund Me" Account to assist in the transport of your body back to Brazil. After completing this and sharing it, it felt like my phone consistently rang for the next 12 hours of that day. Each phone call would be someone screaming to find out what happened to you. I remember one lady who demanded to know where you were and the location of your body. When I had asked how she knew you, she simply advised that she was one of your followers. I immediately advised I would be disconnecting and I would provide any updates to your family. The next phone call was a lady from New Jersey, Lisa, who was hysterical as well. She advised that she had been a very good friend of yours, and that you had visited her several times in the past year. She advised she would be giving a good friend of both of yours my number so she could reach out.

 The next lady who called would be a lady who fought so hard to ensure you were brought home and your legacy was protected. This lady named Mel called me and advised me how she had known you. She was also crying. She advised she had hosted a reality show with you here in Orlando. I immediately remembered you telling me about this reality show and how you really enjoyed the lady who was hosting it. I felt safe talking with her. Mel would advise that whatever I needed, she would work day and night to accomplish it for me. I had brought up the "Go Fund" me account to her, and she advised we would have the $10,000 by the end of the day, and not to worry about money. She advised me to take some time for myself and process everything. She advised she would check in on me later in the day.

The next couple of days, Dany, the girl who helped explain everything to your family and Mel would stay in contact with me every day. They began assisting me with the steps to work with the embassy to ensure we were moving forward in the correct manner. The few days after your death seem like a blur of phone calls and responses to give updates on what we had to do to arrange for your body to go to the funeral home and then complete the necessary paperwork for your flight home. I began receiving calls and messages from random people asking if I could explain what happened and explain the circumstances around your body. I remember I even had a message requesting I come to Salt Lake City to sit down and tell the story of what happened. I began disregarding all these messages as I felt the situation concerning your body and your death were not necessary to the public at this time, but just your family and close friends.

I continued providing updates to your family as requested and finally received the phone call that the police had completed the inspection on your body and were providing it to the funeral home. I remember I told my family that I needed to see you. We took a trip up to Georgia one early morning so we could complete the necessary paperwork and I could see you for the first time. I remember that entire trip I sat in complete silence. Upon arriving at the funeral home, it was the hardest walk of my life to walk into the building in which I knew your body was located. As we sat down with the funeral director, they advised of the next steps with the Embassy to have your body taken home. I remember he made a comment concerning the road-rash you had suffered and I was immediately brought to tears. The funeral director apologized as he just wanted to make sure I was aware of what I was walking into.

As I walked into the room in which you were located, I felt numb. I had asked everyone to leave the room so I could have some time to speak with you. I would tell you how much your family and friends loved you. I would talk about how so many people were fighting to get you home. I talked about how you were the perfect person for me and that even though we would not be able to have the family we talked about, I would still name one of my children after you. I remember I could not stop talking to you. I just wanted you to know how much I loved you and how much you changed my world. I remember after an extended time, my mom had come into the room to check on me. I continued talking to you and holding your hand through the blanket. Finally, I gave you a kiss goodbye and I made a promise I would ensure we kept fighting for you until you were finally able to rest in peace.

As we were driving home from Georgia, I received a call from Mel that she had a contact with the Brazilian Embassy that would assist us in the timely resolution of your paperwork if I was able to bring it to Atlanta. Two days later, once your death certificate was ready, I would make the trip back to Georgia with your friend Dany to ensure we got the needed paperwork and brought it to the Embassy. Upon finally getting to the Embassy with the paperwork, my heart stopped again. Dany helped interpret what was needed next and we waited for about 30 minutes as they processed your paperwork. Upon receiving it back, we drove it back to Savannah Georgia to ensure we could book your flights home timely.

Over the next few days we would wait again to hear if your flight was approved and ready. Throughout these days, I would hear beautiful stories from your friends Dany and Ryan whom I finally got to meet. Ryan was one of your close friends for years who lived in Orlando. I remember you had told me in February that you wanted us to meet. It brought some peace being able to converse with people who knew you on a deeper level and hear similar stories of how you acted when you were with me. One thing that was a recurring theme was that you were an intense personality, you were stubborn, and you were passionate. I would laugh hearing stories about how you drove other people crazy as much as you would drive me crazy. I finally obtained the call that you were approved to go back to Brazil. It was a bit of a hard call for me as it seemed official that you were finally leaving. However, it became heartwarming how grateful everyone was for the fact that you could finally come home.

I would consistently obtain messages from your family about how grateful they were for Dany and I for the daily fighting to ensure you were brought home timely. One that really hit hard was a message from your dad in which he shared on social media how he would be forever grateful for both Dany and I. I remember I had a friend reach out to me to advise how unique it was that a Brazilian father would be so accepting and loving of his son's boyfriend.

The final battle in my heart would now be to attend your funeral. My family and even your friends have been very hesitant on me traveling to Brazil due to the media attention that had occurred around your death. One of your friends recommended I travel with a security guard to assist with my travel to your funeral. It began to worry me a little bit as well. However, I felt if I did not go to your funeral to say goodbye, it would be something that I regret for the rest of my life.

The day before leaving for Brazil, I was going to get gas for our trip to Miami the next day for our flight. As I pulled into the gas station, I saw a large white truck with a trailer attached. I immediately broke into tears. I just pictured you were there in spirit. You were telling me that I was okay to go to Brazil and that you would make sure I was safe. As I pulled in for gas, I kept looking at this man and his truck as he was pumping his gas. I think he saw me keep looking back and forth at him as well. I went and pulled some cash out of my car to give him to assist with his gas. I walked up to him and realized he only spoke Spanish. I walked back to my car and got my phone. I wrote to him that my partner had passed away two weeks ago while driving a truck almost identical to his. I advised him I wanted to help him pay for his gas and that he needed to travel safe. I wrote that I hope God blesses him on this trip and in life. He became so thankful and apologized for my loss. I gave him the money and shook his hand. As I walked away, I knew you were there with both of us smiling down.

On Tuesday morning, I will begin my trip to Brazil to say my final goodbyes to you. I hope you know I love you deeply and you have forever changed my world. You are my greatest love story that began with a knock at 11PM.

www.ingramcontent.com/pod-product-compliance
Lightning Source LLC
LaVergne TN
LVHW011850060526
838200LV00054B/4265